HISTORY OF THE BREED

Small white-coated dogs have been known to man for thousands of years and are likely the ancestors of many of today's small, full-coated, mostly white dog breeds. The Bichon Frise, sometimes called the Tenerife Bichon, can be said, without stretching or revising history too much, to be related loosely in this way to the "little white dogs of antiquity."

As civilizations rose and fell and man extended his dominion from the known and civilized world westward from the eastern Mediterranean, he took his little white companion dogs with him. Eventually these little fellows found their way to such western outposts as the Balearic Islands (Majorca and Minorca), then traveled through Gibraltar to the great beyond of the Canary Islands off the west coast of Africa. We don't know exactly when, how, or in what numbers they arrived but it must have been well into the second millennium, as the original inhabitants of the Canaries were large wild dogs. The best guess is about 1300 AD, and the Tenerife dog or Canary Bichon is thought to be one of the "little white dogs" from that time.

Even though the evidence of their stay in the Canaries is sketchy at best, it is known that these small white dogs, later known as Tenerife Bichons or Tenerife terriers (named for the

The first breed standard for the Bichon was written by the Toy Club of France with the help of a Belgian breeders' association. Sarah, Sidonie, and Quetty are three Bichons that were owned by prominent French breeder Mme. Laisne.

largest Canary Island), were brought back from the Canaries to western Europe. The "when" is lost in the sands of time, but it was certainly during and just after the age of discovery in the late 15th and early 16th centuries. It is known that small, fluffy-coated, white dogs whose immediate ancestors were brought back to Europe by merchants, traders, and navigators bred true to type when bred in local isolation and became popular, identifiable, regional breeds. They often took the name of their region or city-state in the late Middle Ages. These regional breeds of small dogs, or bichons, are sometimes lumped together as a family called the bichon family.

The Maltese is one of the small, fluffy white dogs that was recognized as a member of the bichon family.

The Tenerife Bichon remained an identifiable and separate dog that was distinguishable from the other bichon family members such as the Maltese and other small, mostly white, fluffy dogs. There were family members in the New World (particularly South America and Cuba) as well as on the continent of Europe. Indeed there is sufficient reason to believe that until well into the 20th century, when the term "Bichon Frise" was invented, just about all 19th century look-alikes were Tenerife Bichons—ancestor dogs of today's Bichon Frise whatever their size and shape, even if they were called by other names.

Certainly there was considerable crossbreeding, either intentional or unintentional, with other bichon relatives, so it is also fair to say that the contemporary Bichon Frise is a blend of many bichon regional types that descended from the little, mostly white dogs of antiquity and that were separated throughout the ages into distinct regional types as man spread across the globe into different geographical locations. Each offshoot was bred in isolation and then, in the modern age of international communication and contact, reunited in a glorious blend that produced the handsome Bichon Frise.

One thing is certain—the Bichon Frise has a definite historical connection with the Canary Islands and Tenerife, the Canaries' largest principal island. The term "Bichon Frise" apparently was employed for the first time in reference to those

Illustrations of the Bichon in the 19th century depict a dog that resembles the Bichon Frise of today.

Tenerife Bichons meeting a new standard of type in 1933. The official standard of the breed was adopted on March 15th of that year and was written by the president of the Toy Club of France in cooperation with a Belgian breeders' association. It was named for its appearance—Bichon Frise translates into "fluffy little dog." However, for many years this "new breed" continued to be classified alternatively as "the Tenerife dog" or the Bichon à Poil Frisé (bichon of the curly hair).

The Bichon Frise existed largely in its present form long before 1933; it was just called by other names. The Bichon was popular as a house pet and lap dog of the gentry in the late 19th century, both in England and western Europe. Nineteenth century oil paintings and portraits of the rich and famous have depicted bichons remarkably similar to today's Bichon Frise. He appears now and then in impressionistic art as a floating image at the beach or as a child's companion in a portrait. However, as all human endeavors seem to move in cycles, so do matters of taste. It befell the Bichon to lose favor with the Beau Monde at the end of the 19th century, passing into the hands of the less fortunate orders of society and becoming the dog of the street entertainer and the house pet of the obscure. This was especially true in Belgium and France.

As with other breeds after World War I, breed fanciers and dog lovers of the leisure class in France and Belgium resurrected the Bichon from the ashes of the Great War and years of indifferent breeding as the "dog of the streets." Intelligent, careful breeding of the Tenerife Bichons or Bichons à Poil Frisés, as they were identified by the dog fanciers engaged in the project, resulted by 1933 in sufficient consistency to warrant writing a breed standard. The resulting dog, the Bichon Frise, can be therefore said to be a dog of Franco-Belgian

In the late 19th century, the Bichon Frise was a popular high-society house pet throughout England and western Europe.

origin. This "new breed" developed through foundation stock of the Tenerife dog, or Tenerife Bichon, which was in itself an ancient dog that traced back to the "little white dogs" of antiquity known to the seafaring civilizations of the eastern Mediterranean.

Who would have thought back in 1933, when the first French standard was developed, that this little, white, fluffy dog would in 60 years become a popular favorite world-wide with thousands of admirers, would be recognized by national kennel clubs, and would be given full breed recognition?

THE BICHON IN AMERICA

This sudden huge burst of popularity is largely owed to the introduction of the Bichon Frise into the US. While many Americans traveling on the Continent had brought back bichons of one type or another for decades, the first documented arrival of a specimen of the breed that met the French standard for the Bichon Frise was in 1956. It took just 17 years for the Bichon to receive full breed recognition from the American Kennel Club. It was through the efforts of a few dedicated and determined partisans operating with a singleness of purpose that this was accomplished. While the first Bichons were introduced in the Milwaukee area, circumstances saw the center of promotional or breeding activity shifted to southern California, chiefly San Diego. In May of 1964, the Bichon Frise Club of America was formed. This club, comprised largely of California and Wisconsin residents at first, became the driving force for the rapid acceptance of the Bichon Frise by the AKC. Later, local groups of Bichon clubs formed in other areas of the country and contributed to the effort. The Bichon's enormous popularity in the US, and ultimately their international popularity, is owed directly to the efforts of these early clubs.

The fluffy white dog known as the Bichon Frise enjoyed a phenomenal burst of popularity, largely due to its introduction into the United States.

The first match shows were held during the mid-1960s. At this time, there was no general consensus about grooming or show presentation. Bichons had appeared after the war in European show rings but they were usually ungroomed and presented "as is" in a fashion that US dog fancier circles, including the AKC, considered unkempt. Unfortunately, Bichons were viewed with skepticism by US judges, breeders, and others of prominence in America whose image of the Bichon was colored by the rather crude unwashed, uncut, and unbrushed version of the Bichon being shown in Europe. Whatever the merits of grooming as it contributes to form rather than function, those determined to secure AKC recognition for the Bichon realized early on that the stereotypical image of the Bichon had to be changed. No amount of righteous railing against snobbery and false values, based upon grooming that conceals the dogs' soundness, would change things and allow the Bichon to take its rightful place as an equal of other fully recognized "pure breeds."

European Bichons were usually shown "as is"—grooming was considered unimportant. Ch. Lola des Closmyons, a Bichon bred and owned by Mme. Laisne of France, displays the typical European look.

In the 1960s, great emphasis began to be placed on grooming, which was promoted with the aid of regional seminars sponsored by those working toward the Bichon's AKC recognition. The grooming "standard" was gradually hammered out, resulting in the fully rounded fluffy look that evolved over time into the orthodox "look" of today's Bichons.

Brochures were printed and distributed by the Bichon Club of America, Inc, to promote the new look. This was a large step toward AKC recognition and helped overcome the stereotypical picture of the little street dog still prevalent in the minds of many of those influential in the canine world. Further, in the late 1960s, the assistance of well-connected individuals, including the editor of a leading dog publication, was successfully enlisted. Gradually, every obstacle was overcome. The Bichon's popularity grew, resulting in far greater geographical distribution across the US.

In addition to the increase in the number of dogs and people involved with Bichons, there was increasing uniformity and adherence to the standard. This was fostered partially by the aforementioned grooming campaign and the efforts of the local clubs that proliferated during this period. This in turn resulted in more interest and promotional activities at the local level including, most importantly, match shows.

By the early 1970s, the efforts of selective breeding fostered by the publicity and promotional campaigns of the early Bichon enthusiasts had resulted not only in increased uniformity but also in improved conformation and, depending on one's opinion, improved overall quality of the hardy little dog. All of this work paid off handsomely in 1971 when the AKC accepted the Bichon Frise in the Miscellaneous Class. Two years later in 1973, the Bichon Frise achieved full breed recognition.

All of this was accomplished in just 17 years from the time the first Bichons Frises were brought into the US. This was a remarkable accomplishment and a tribute to the perseverance of the early Bichon Frise partisans. Not the least of their accomplishments was the acceptance of the Bichon Frise by the AKC into the Non-Sporting Group as opposed to the Toy Group. This grouping is peculiar to the US, as "toy" is the world-wide classification adopted by almost

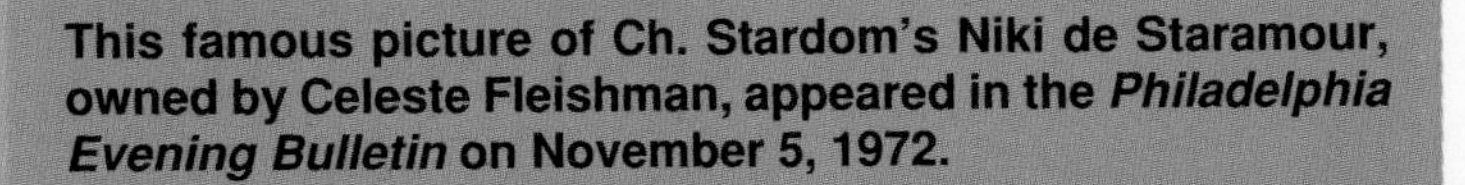

This famous picture of Ch. Stardom's Niki de Staramour, owned by Celeste Fleishman, appeared in the *Philadelphia Evening Bulletin* on November 5, 1972.

every other national and international registration body.

The position of the American breeders was that the size restriction of the Toy Group would not give full expression to the true nature of the breed. The Bichon Frise and his predecessors in the Canaries and other remote parts of the world had been tough little fellows made even hardier in later centuries as street and carnival performers, albeit with time out for a while as lap companions of the aristocrats. To have survived more or less intact with only a few changes over the ages suggests that the Bichon Frise is no "toy" by any means.

The first American breed standard for the Bichon was hammered out by the early charter members of the Bichon Frise Club of America in 1964. This was modified and adopted by an expanded membership four years later in 1968. In 1974, the year after full breed recognition, the AKC approved this standard as the official standard for the breed. Bichon popularity grew rapidly, and the breed began to appear in shows across the nation with such frequency and in such numbers that an all-Bichon Frise specialty show was sponsored by the Bichon Frise Club of America in 1976.

A further modification of the breed standard was made in 1979 due to the problem of disparate judging by judges who were offered considerable latitude by perceived ambiguities in the standard. The newness of the breed, along with the preconceived conceptions of some judges, sometimes resulted in

The American grooming campaign resulted in a fluffy, fully rounded look that eventually became the accepted look for the modern Bichon.

decisions that seemed at odds with the goals of the breeders' association. Because of these special circumstances, the Bichon standard, which would seem sufficiently specific for most breeds, was deemed too loose. A more detailed and more specific standard was worked up by the club and approved by the AKC as the official standard for conformation in 1979. This is the basis of the present day Bichon Frise standard. In harmony with a general AKC standardization drive for all recognized breeds, a further minor modification was needed and adopted in 1988. This last modification brought about the standard that is in force today.

AMERICAN INFLUENCE AROUND THE WORLD

Curiously, the Bichon Frise known for generations in Europe, both in its present form and as its earlier near relations, only became universally popular after its meteoric rise to popularity in the US. The American influence has had a profound effect on the Bichon Frise establishment the world over, including France and Belgium which are considered the Bichon's countries of origin and the places that gave the breed its name. This influence has extended even to modifications of the breed standards, or in the alternative, ignoring the local standard and embracing the

Bichons compete successfully in all aspects of the dog sport—Ch. Chateau's Idealbo Rivage d'Ami, CDX, is a conformation champion and the first male Bichon to earn the CD title.

American ideals, particularly in the area of grooming. There is even a point of view with a respectable following that holds that the modern Bichon Frise as we know it has, in the last few decades, changed and evolved so much as to be quite separate and distinct from those brought to the US in 1956 from the Continent, and thus is an American creation or an "American breed."

Today Bichons Frises compete successfully at major shows all over the world. They have more than held their own and have won Bests in Show at many world class shows, and they have done well in the Non-Sporting Group at the Westminster show at Madison Square Garden in New York.

The American influence was immediate, widespread, and dominant. In 1975, two years after full American recognition by the AKC, the Canadian Kennel Club followed the American example and placed the Bichon in the Non-Sporting Group. The Canadian standard was adopted in 1975 and it was strongly influenced by the American standard observed at that time. The standard adopted was largely the work of a committee of Bichon breeders. However, the Canadian Kennel Club, as in almost every country except the US, considered this merely as a recommendation or advisory and reserved the right to introduce their own concepts into the standard. This was done accordingly in due course, and the composite was adopted as the standard in 1975. This standard is still in force today in Canada.

The American influence in England is obvious. There were no known Bichons Frises in England until the year of official AKC recognition in 1973. That same year saw the first importation of Bichons by an English breeder. Greater numbers were imported the following year, many from the US. By 1976, there were enough dogs, breeders, and owners to form the Bichon Frise Club of Great Britain. The first all-Bichon Frise championship show was held in 1982, the same year that strong regional geographical clubs were formed. The English dogs bred in the 1970s and early 1980s were a mix of American and continental bloodlines. The blend has continued up to this day with more modern continental lines modifying the original American-dominant gene pool. Some of the resulting bloodlines have been reintroduced into US breeding programs in a sort of reverse migration.

The American influence on the Bichon Frise in England is apparent. Eng. Ch. Sibon Fatal Attraction at Pamplona is a top award winner and record holder in the UK and is the first Bichon to be awarded "Dog of the Year."

The "American," or highly groomed, version of the Bichon Frise became popular all over the world. Europe, Scandinavia, Australia, and Japan are just a few of the places where the Bichon's new look has caught on.

Other places where the "new" Bichon Frise was introduced, took root, and became popular were Sweden in 1976, Australia in the same year, and New Zealand in 1977. Japan offers another example of the American influence. The first Bichon introduced into Japan came from France in 1970, three years before AKC or US recognition. Interestingly, the Japanese Kennel Club recognized the Bichon Frise in 1972, a year before full recognition by the AKC. At that time, the AKC gave only modified recognition as a rare breed to the Bichon. The American influence really hit home after 1975 when Japanese delegates visiting the US saw the "American" or "new" highly groomed Bichon at American shows. This type quickly became the dog of choice in Japan and a flurry of importation took place, making the dog a popular favorite numbering in the thousands. A curious phenomenon has been the see-saw Group classification of the Bichon by the Japanese Kennel Club. At first the Bichon was classified in the Toy Group. In 1977, obviously influenced by the American experience, the Japanese Kennel Club adopted the practice of the AKC and put the Bichon in the Non-Sporting Group. There he remained until 1988, when the Japanese Kennel Club adopted the Federation Cynologique Internationale (FCI) standard (the modern standard of France and Belgium) and was obliged under that standard to return the Bichon to the Toy Group. By the mid-1980s there were sufficient Bichons Frises in Japan to hold specialty shows.

As noted, Bichons were first imported to Sweden from the US in 1976. Bichons are also found in the other Scandinavian countries of Denmark and Norway. They are abundant in western Europe, including Germany, Holland, Switzerland, and, of course, Belgium and France (which have a substantial claim to place of origin). There is also considerable interest in Bichons in Ireland, Scotland, and especially Mexico.

These were the countries represented at the first international Bichon Frise Congress that was held in London, England in 1988. This convention of owners, breeders, and sponsors of the breed was a gathering of parties with a mutual

The Bichon Frise became especially popular in Japan, where the Japanese Kennel Club recognized the breed a year before the American Kennel Club did.

The first international Bichon Frise Congress was held in London in 1988. Grooming was a highly debated topic—American fanciers favored the fully groomed rounded look while the French preferred the ungroomed "as is" look.

interest in improving, promoting, and defining this relatively "young" breed. This congress, really a "gentle" international conference, was unique and unprecedented for any breed. It was hosted by the Bichon Frise Club of Great Britain. The fact that an international meeting of Bichon people could be held successfully 15 years after AKC recognition shows how high and fast the fame and fortune of the Bichon Frise had risen from a little-known French dog and rare descendant of an ancient breed to a "nouveau" quasi-American breed with an international following.

One interesting subject before the convention was the issue of grooming. The American delegates and many others put forth their strong opinions that it was grooming and the resultant improvement in presentation that was the root of the fantastic change in the Bichon's fortune. Indeed, it was their view that if it weren't for grooming and the chain reaction thereafter set off from America, there would be no Congress and many present would never have heard of the Bichon Frise. Grooming demonstrations were given by the partisans of this point of view and were generally well received by most attendees, including those from France and other nations which used the FCI standard. The FCI is based in France. Their standard, used by several nations, requires that Bichons Frises be shown "as is" without brushing, clipping, and last minute bathing that disturbs the natural lie of the coat. It is an offshoot of the original French standard that some "purists" feel preserves the essence of the breed. To the FCI, grooming is a process that over-emphasizes form over function and helps hide defects that reduce a dog's soundness. To them, grooming is a step toward the eventual disintegration and downfall of the breed because it emphasizes show form for commercial purposes, which after a chain of events could lead to mass indiscriminate breeding. Those with the opposing point of view claim with considerable justification that today's Bichon is a sounder, better dog that can meet the most exacting and sharply defined standard in the world—the American standard. The first Bichon congress did indeed pass a resolution suggesting that Bichon clubs petition the FCI for a change in policy. Even at shows in countries using the FCI standard, Bichon Frise exhibitors and judges frequently turn a blind eye and the dogs are shown fully groomed just like in the US.

Int-Can-Monaco Ch. Ami's Rick de Neigenuvieaux enjoyed a brilliant show career in France. There has always been considerable interest in Bichons in France and Belgium, as these countries are considered the breed's places of origin.

DESCRIPTION OF THE BREED

The Bichon, reflecting his history as a hardy, long-lived little breed, is an ideal companion. He enjoys an excellent reputation as an all-around family dog. A well-known breeder in Pennsylvania, who has at one time or another bred or had contact with 17 different breeds, ranks the Bichon as the best all-around small, non-shedding, family dog with an ideal temperament. His small size has made the Bichon Frise a great favorite with apartment dwellers and others with limited living space. When properly groomed, the Bichon seems to strut with a gait that can be a joy to watch as well as a source of great amusement.

Bichons become very strongly attached to their people, which can be a problem, especially for owners who have to leave their pets unattended for more than a few hours at a time. This also holds true for those who travel a lot and need to leave pets behind in kennels or in temporary foster care (even for a few days). The Bichon is prone to separation anxiety and may pine away or bark continuously during your absence. This can have an adverse long-range effect on his temperament. Frequent episodes

The Bichon Frise's friendly, outgoing disposition and even temperament make him an ideal companion. He is considered by many to be the best choice for an all-around family dog.

Although not considered a toy breed, the Bichon is still small enough to adapt to limited living quarters. This pair of tiny young Bichons is a basket full of puppy love!

can create a pet that is highly excitable and even moderately aggressive toward strangers. Great care should be taken to introduce the little dog to being alone for any length of time. This should be done in stages by gradually increasing the intervals of separation and slowly conditioning him to your absence. A blanket, stuffed toy, or article of clothing that has your familiar bouquet will go a long way toward reassuring him.

Fortunately, the Bichon Frise is easy to train, and you can overcome this problem and many other potential trouble spots, including aggression, with good, sound, intelligent training. It is fair to say that many problems associated with the temperament of the Bichon as well as other breeds are caused by inexperience and lack of knowledge on the owner's part. When properly trained and nurtured, a happy healthy Bichon has a sunny outgoing disposition. If he can be made to feel secure and loved, he will reward his people with boundless affection.

The temperament of the well-adjusted Bichon is so exceptionally good for a small breed that he is used as a therapy dog at hospitals and old age homes. Bichons have been used successfully to bring comfort to children, the elderly, convalescents, and the handicapped. Only dogs with very stable temperaments are suited for this type of work. The dogs must not only be very friendly but also able to adapt to the unusual

It's no surprise that the Bichon Frise excels at agility. His high trainability and inherent knack for performing make him a natural at this fun, yet demanding, dog sport.

circumstances of the facilities they visit. Only a dog that is very trainable and capable of reacting and responding to the required commands is suitable for therapy work. Bichon Frise regional clubs cooperate fully with voluntary organizations that provide therapy dogs for this purpose. They have found that the small size and loving temperament of the Bichon make him an ideal therapy dog.

The Bichon is so highly trainable that he has excelled in competitions requiring a high degree of training and conditioning. Bichons have performed well and more than held their own in obedience trials, which is a remarkable accomplishment for a small dog. This may well be a throwback to the late 19th century when the Bichon Frise, then known as the Tenerife Bichon, was the dog of the organ grinder, the circus performer, and the street entertainer. The Bichon is not a fragile little lap dog and is quite correctly placed in the Non-

Although no longer a circus act or a street performer, the Bichon still loves to entertain with his playful strut and amusing antics.

The best prospective Bichon owner is one who understands the breed and is committed to the dog's proper care and upbringing. Your Bichon puppy will grow up to give you a lifetime of love and loyalty—he deserves the best!

Sporting Group by the American Kennel Club (AKC). However, this doesn't mean that he is no "sport." In addition to obedience, Bichons have done well in such AKC and regional club events as tracking, agility, and weight pulling. These feats are a tribute to the Bichon's high degrees of trainability and responsiveness.

The prospective Bichon owner should learn all he can about the Bichon before buying one. He can call a local regional Bichon club and get valuable information about the breed and breeders. A properly informed buyer can decide whether or not the Bichon is a good choice. If the decision is yes, knowledge about the breed will help him in finding a puppy. Armed with the right information, the new owner has what he needs to raise his Bichon the right way and to avoid the mistakes common to those who don't understand the breed. To understand the Bichon Frise is to love him—he is one of the best breeds known to man.

STANDARD FOR THE BREED

A breed standard is the criterion by which the appearance (and to a certain extent, the temperament as well) of any given dog is made subject to objective measurement. Basically, the standard for any breed is a definition of the perfect dog to which all specimens of the breed are compared. Breed standards are always subject to change through review by the national breed club for each dog, so that it is always wise to keep up with developments in a breed by checking the publications of your national kennel club.

The Bichon's "merry temperament," as called for in the standard, should be evident in his facial expression. This happy Bichon is "merry" personified!

AKC STANDARD FOR THE BICHON FRISE

General Appearance—The Bichon Frise is a small, sturdy, white powder puff of a dog whose merry temperament is evidenced by his plumed tail carried jauntily over the back and his dark-eyed inquisitive expression.

This is a breed that has no gross or incapacitating exaggerations and therefore there is no inherent reason for lack of balance or unsound movement.

Any deviation from the ideal described in the standard should be penalized to the extent of the deviation. Structural faults common to all breeds are as undesirable in the Bichon Frise as in any other breed, even though such faults may not be specifically mentioned in the standard.

Size, Proportion, Substance—***Size***—Dogs and bitches 9 $^1/_2$ to 11 $^1/_2$ inches are to be given primary preference. Only where the comparative superiority of a specimen outside this range clearly justifies it should greater latitude be taken. In no case, however, should this latitude ever extend over 12 inches or under 9 inches. The minimum limits do not apply to puppies. ***Proportion***—The body from the forward-most point of the chest to the point of rump is $^1/_4$ longer than the height at the withers. The body from the withers to the lowest point of the chest represents $^1/_2$ the distance from withers to ground. ***Substance***—Compact and of medium bone throughout; neither coarse nor fine.

Head—***Expression***—Soft, dark-eyed, inquisitive, alert. ***Eyes*** are round, black or dark brown and are set in the skull to look directly forward. An overly large or bulging eye is a fault as is an almond shaped, obliquely set eye. Halos, the black or very dark brown skin surrounding the eyes, are necessary as they accentuate the eye and enhance expression. The eye rims themselves must be black. Broken pigment, or total absence of pigment on the eye rims produce a blank and staring expression, which is a definite fault. Eyes of any color other than black or dark brown are a very serious fault and must be severely penalized. ***Ears*** are drop and are covered with long flowing hair. When extended toward the nose, the leathers reach approximately halfway the length of the muzzle. They are set on slightly higher than eye level and rather forward on the skull, so that when the dog is alert they serve to frame the face. The ***skull*** is slightly rounded, allowing for a round and forward looking eye. The ***stop*** is slightly accentuated. ***Muzzle***—A properly balanced head is three parts muzzle to five parts skull, measured from the nose to the stop and from the stop to the occiput. A line drawn between the outside corners of the eyes and to the nose will create a near equilateral triangle. There is a slight degree of chiseling under the eyes, but not so much as to result in a weak or snipey foreface. The lower jaw is strong. The ***nose*** is prominent and always black. ***Lips*** are black, fine, never drooping. ***Bite*** is scissors. A bite which is undershot or overshot should be severely penalized. A crooked or out of line tooth is permissible, however, missing teeth are to be severely faulted.

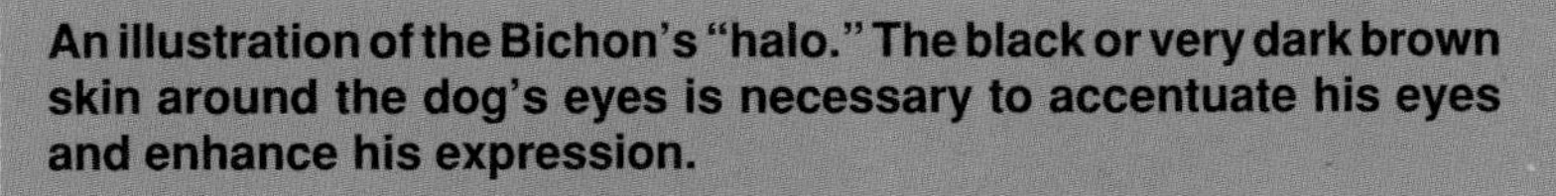

An illustration of the Bichon's "halo." The black or very dark brown skin around the dog's eyes is necessary to accentuate his eyes and enhance his expression.

Neck, Topline and Body—The arched ***neck*** is long and carried proudly behind an erect head. It blends smoothly into the shoulders. The length of neck from

The Bichon's attitude can be seen in the jaunty carriage of his tail. The well-plumed tail should be held in a graceful curve over the back so that the hair of the tail rests on the back.

occiput to withers is approximately $^1/_3$ the distance from forechest to buttocks. The ***topline*** is level except for a slight, muscular arch over the loin. ***Body***—The chest is well developed and wide enough to allow free and unrestricted movement of the front legs. The lowest point of the chest extends at least to the elbow. The rib cage is moderately sprung and extends back to a short and muscular loin. The forechest is well pronounced and protrudes slightly forward of the point of shoulder. The underline has a moderate tuck-up. The ***tail*** is well plumed, set on level with the topline and curved gracefully over the back so that the hair of the tail rests on the back. When the tail is extended toward the head it reaches at least halfway to the withers. A low tail set, a tail carried perpendicularly to the back, or a tail which droops behind is to be severely penalized. A corkscrew tail is a very serious fault.

Forequarters—*Shoulders*— The shoulder blade, upper arm and forearm are approximately equal in length. The shoulders are laid back to somewhat near a forty-five degree angle. The upper arm extends well back so the elbow is placed directly below the withers when viewed from the side. ***Legs*** are of medium bone; straight, with no bow or curve in the forearm or wrist. The elbows are held close to the body. The ***pasterns*** slope slightly from the vertical. The dewclaws may be removed. The ***feet*** are tight and round, resembling those of a cat and point directly forward, turning neither in nor out. The ***pads*** are black. ***Nails*** are kept short.

Hindquarters—The hindquarters are of medium bone, well angulated with muscular thighs and spaced moderately wide. The upper and lower thigh are nearly equal in length meeting at a well bent stifle joint. The leg from hock joint to foot pad is perpendicular to the ground. Dewclaws may be removed. Paws are tight and round with black pads.

Coat—The texture of the coat is of utmost importance. The undercoat is soft and dense, the outercoat of a coarser and curlier texture. The combination of the two gives a soft but substantial feel to the touch which is similar to plush or velvet and when patted springs back. When bathed and brushed, it stands off the body, creating an overall powder puff appearance. A wiry coat is not desirable. A limp, silky coat, a coat that lies down, or a lack of undercoat are very serious faults. ***Trimming***—The coat is trimmed to reveal the natural outline of the body. It is rounded off from any direction and never cut so short as to create an overly trimmed or squared off appearance. The furnishings of the head, beard, moustache, ears and tail are left longer. The longer head hair is trimmed to create an overall rounded impression. The topline is trimmed to appear level. The coat is long enough to maintain the powder puff look which is characteristic of the breed.

Color—Color is white, may have shadings of buff, cream or apricot around the ears or on the body. Any color in excess of 10% of the entire coat of a mature specimen is a fault and should be penalized, but color of the accepted shadings should not be faulted in puppies.

Gait—Movement at a trot is free, precise and effortless. In profile the forelegs and hind legs extend equally with an easy reach and drive that maintain a steady topline. When moving, the head and neck remain somewhat erect and as speed increases there is a very slight convergence of legs toward the center line. Moving away, the hindquarters travel with moderate width between them and the foot pads can be seen. Coming and going, his movement is precise and true.

Temperament—Gentle mannered, sensitive, playful and affectionate. A cheerful attitude is the hallmark of the breed and one should settle for nothing less.

COMMENTS ON THE STANDARD

No standard is more specific and descriptive than the American standard, which has been modified and refined over time to meet this objective. It compares most favorably with the best-written standards of any AKC breed. It stresses soundness.

Dogs and bitches are to be between 9 and 12 inches at the

A properly groomed and trimmed Bichon coat should follow the outline of the body and have an overall "powder puff" look. The facial furnishings are left longer to create a distinct rounded appearance.

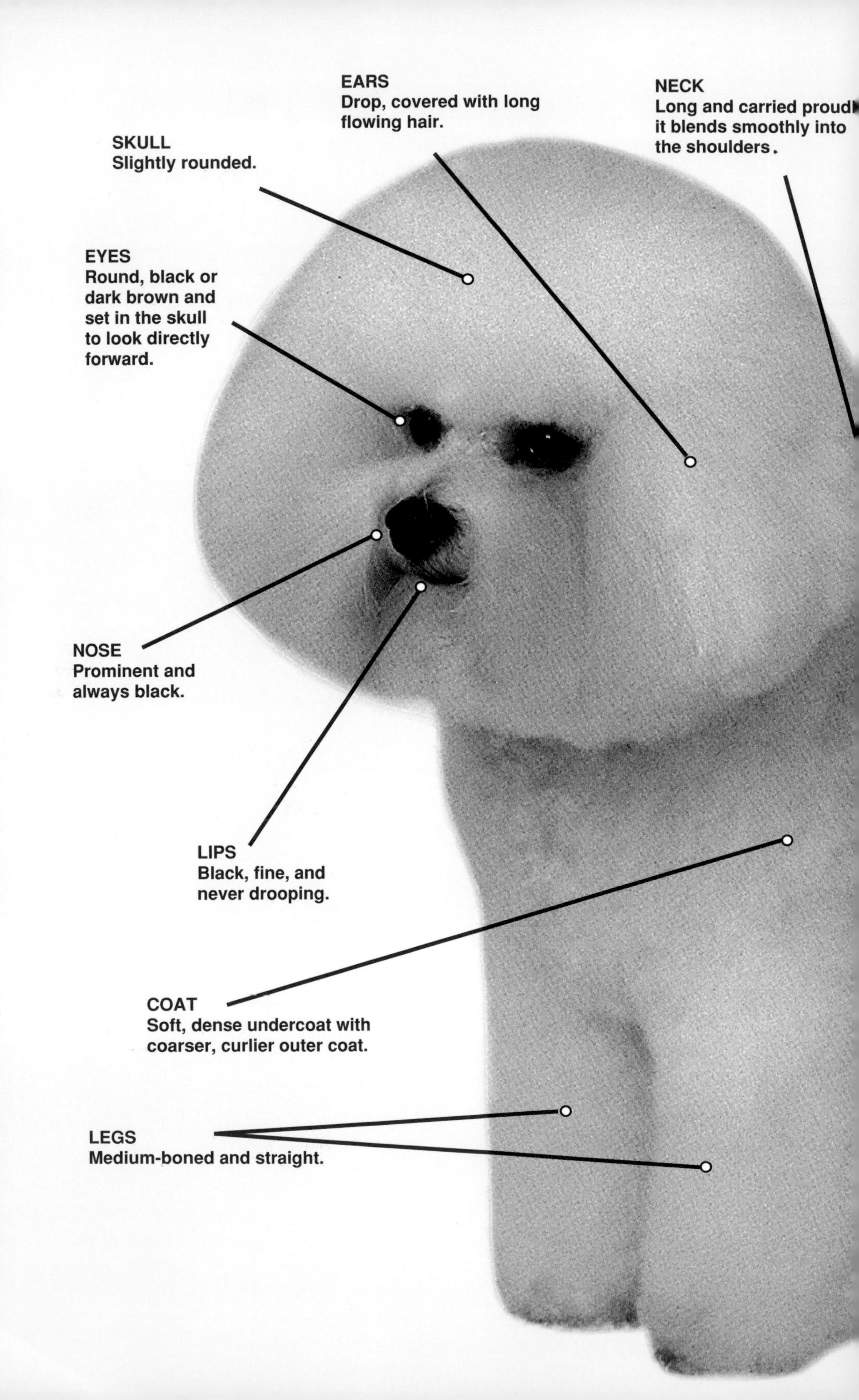
EARS
Drop, covered with long flowing hair.
NECK
Long and carried proudl
it blends smoothly into the shoulders.
SKULL
Slightly rounded.
EYES
Round, black or dark brown and set in the skull to look directly forward.
NOSE
Prominent and always black.
LIPS
Black, fine, and never drooping.
COAT
Soft, dense undercoat with coarser, curlier outer coat.
LEGS
Medium-boned and straight.

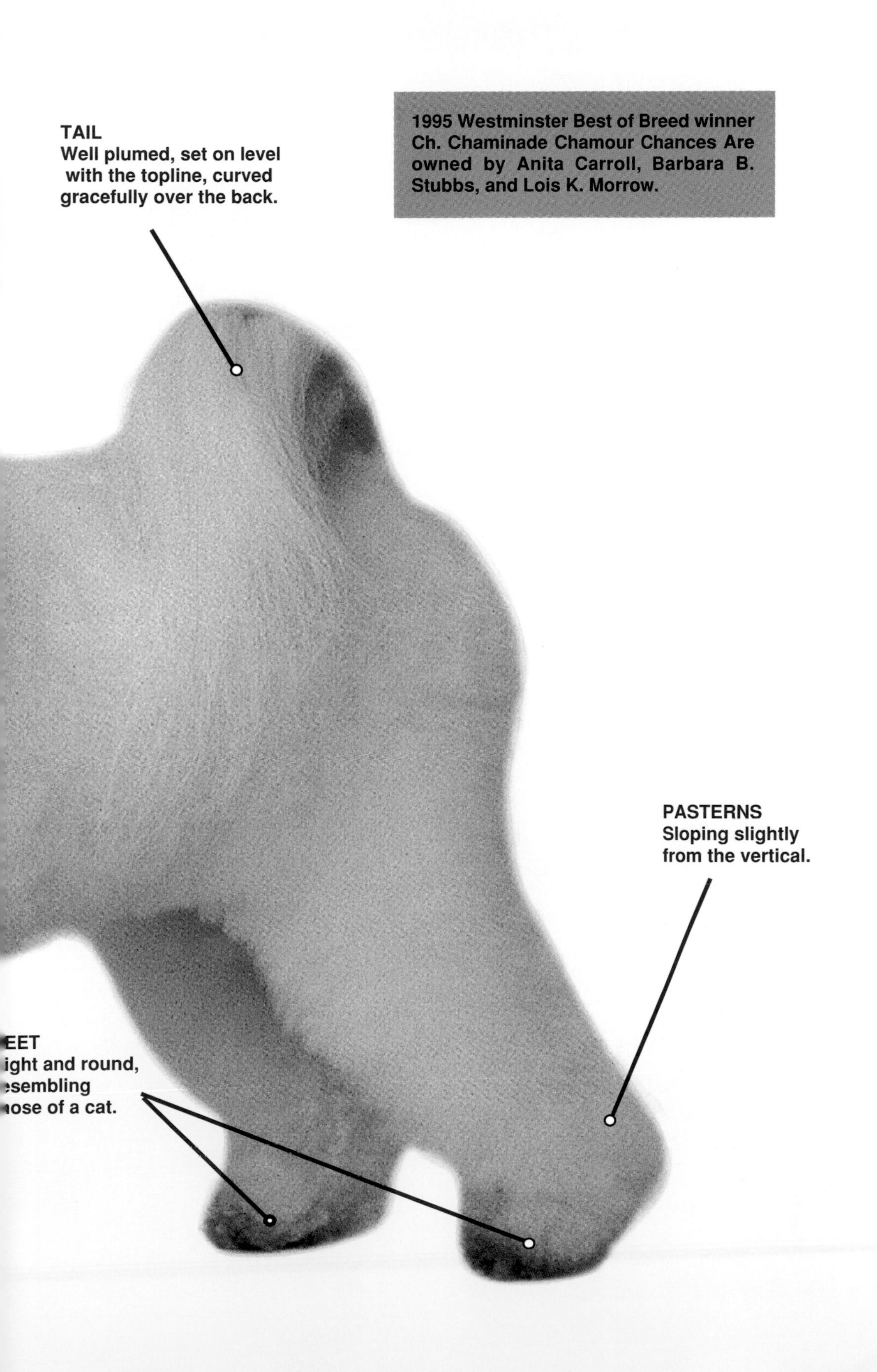

1995 Westminster Best of Breed winner Ch. Chaminade Chamour Chances Are owned by Anita Carroll, Barbara B. Stubbs, and Lois K. Morrow.

withers, with 9 $^1/_2$ to 11 $^1/_2$ inches preferred. The body from the sternum, the most forward part of the chest, to the point of the rump is 25% longer than the height at the withers. The body from the withers to the low point of the chest should be one half of the distance from the withers to the ground. This describes a very sound, sturdy little dog. The length is very specific—it is a step back toward the old French standard and is in exact accordance with the FCI standard (which forbids grooming). Proportion is everything, making size irrelevant as long as it is within the parameters of the standard.

The American standard requires a white coat but allows shades of up to 10% of cream, apricot, or buff. Most other world-wide standards including the British, Australian, and FCI require pure white, and any departure is a point-costing defect.

The Bichon is essentially a white, double-coated breed. There is considerable variance from standard to standard in the description of coat. These differences greatly affect presentation and therefore cross over into the area of grooming. The American standard calls for a soft dense undercoat with an outer coat that is coarser and of a curlier texture. Other standards, notably the Canadian, call for a softer outer coat. The British and Australian standards call for a natural white coat that curls loosely and is patterned after the old French standard that described a fine, silky, and loosely curled outer coat. The FCI standard calls for an outer coat that is fine, silky, corkscrewed, and very slack and only briefly mentions an undercoat.

The Bichon's coat and accepted grooming practices have always been sources of much debate. The American standard calls for a soft dense undercoat with a coarse curly outer coat and favors the precisely groomed "powder puff" look.

YOUR NEW BICHON PUPPY

SELECTION

When you do pick out a Bichon puppy as a pet, don't be hasty; the longer you study puppies, the better you will understand them. Make it your transcendent concern to select only one that radiates good health and spirit and is lively on his feet, whose eyes are bright, whose coat shines, and who comes forward eagerly to make and to cultivate your acquaintance. Don't fall for any shy little darling that wants to retreat to his bed or his box, or plays coy behind other puppies or people, or hides his head under your arm or jacket appealing to your protective instinct. *Pick the Bichon puppy who forthrightly picks you! The feeling of attraction should be mutual!*

DOCUMENTS

Now, a little paper work is in order. When you purchase a purebred Bichon puppy, you should receive a transfer of ownership, registration material, and other "papers" (a list of the immunization shots, if any, the puppy may have been given; a note on whether or not the puppy has been wormed; a diet and feeding schedule to which the puppy is accustomed) and you are

"Take me home...no, over here...pick me!" These Bichons' puppy-dog eyes may be hard to resist, but responsible dog ownership starts with a careful selection based on more than just puppy cuteness.

welcomed as a fellow owner to a long, pleasant association with a most lovable pet, and more (news)paper work.

GENERAL PREPARATION

You have chosen to own a particular Bichon puppy. You have chosen it very carefully over all other breeds and all other puppies. So before you ever get that Bichon puppy home, you will have prepared for its arrival by reading everything you can get your hands on having to do with the management of Bichons and puppies. True, you will run into many conflicting opinions, but at least you will not be starting "blind." Read, study, digest. Talk over your plans with your veterinarian, other "Bichon people," and the seller of your Bichon puppy.

When you get your Bichon puppy, you will find that your reading and study are far from finished. You've just scratched the surface in your plan to provide the greatest possible comfort and health for your Bichon; and, by the same token, you do want to assure yourself of the greatest possible enjoyment of this wonderful creature. You must be ready for this puppy mentally as well as in the physical requirements.

By making the necessary preparations before you bring your Bichon puppy home, you can help make his transition into your home easier.

TRANSPORTATION

If you take the puppy home by car, protect him from drafts, particularly in cold weather. Wrapped in a towel and carried in the arms or lap of a passenger, the Bichon puppy will usually make the trip without mishap. If the pup starts to drool and to squirm, stop the car for a few minutes. Have newspapers handy in case of car-sickness. A covered carton lined with newspapers provides protection for puppy and car, if you are driving alone. Avoid excitement and unnecessary handling of the puppy on arrival. A Bichon puppy is a very small "package" to be making a complete change of surroundings and company, and he needs frequent rest and refreshment to renew his vitality.

THE FIRST DAY AND NIGHT

When your Bichon puppy arrives in your home, put him down on the floor and don't pick him up again, except when it is absolutely necessary. He is a dog, a real dog, and must not be lugged around like a rag doll. Handle him as little as possible, and permit no one to pick him up and baby him. To repeat, *put your Bichon puppy on the floor or the*

The thought of a cute Bichon puppy under the Christmas tree may be tempting, but remember that a puppy is not a toy. A new environment and the excitement of the holidays may be too much for a small puppy to handle all at once.

ground and let him stay there except when it may be necessary to do otherwise.

Quite possibly your Bichon puppy will be afraid for a while in his new surroundings, without his mother and littermates. Comfort him and reassure him, but don't console him. Don't give him the "oh-you-poor-itsy-bitsy-puppy" treatment. Be calm, friendly, and reassuring. Encourage him to walk around and sniff over his new home. If it's dark, put on the lights. Let him roam for a few minutes while you and everyone else concerned sit quietly or go about your routine business. Let the puppy come back to you.

Playmates may cause an immediate problem if the new Bichon puppy is to be greeted by children or other pets. If not, you can skip this subject. The natural affinity between puppies and children calls for some supervision until a live-and-let-live relationship is established. This applies particularly to a Christmas puppy, when there is more excitement than usual and more chance for a puppy to swallow something upsetting. It is a better plan to welcome the puppy several days before or after the holiday week. Like a baby,

A Bichon puppy should be allowed to "sniff around" with proper supervision.

your Bichon puppy needs much rest and should not be over-handled. Once a child realizes that a puppy has "feelings" similar to his own, and can readily be hurt or injured, the opportunities for play and responsibilities provide exercise and training for both.

For his first night with you, he should be put where he is to sleep every night—say in the kitchen, since its floor can usually be easily cleaned. Let him explore the kitchen to his heart's content; close doors to confine him there. Prepare his food and feed him lightly the first night. Give him a pan with some water in it—not a lot, since most puppies will try to drink the whole pan dry. Give him an old coat or shirt to lie on. Since a coat or shirt will be strong in human scent, he will pick it out to lie on, thus furthering his feeling of security in the room where he has just been fed.

HOUSEBREAKING HELPS

Now, sooner or later—mostly sooner—your new Bichon puppy is going to "puddle" on the floor. First take a newspaper and lay it on the puddle until the urine is soaked up onto the paper. *Save this paper.* Now take a cloth with soap and water, wipe up the floor and dry it well. Then take the wet paper and place it on a fairly large square of newspapers in a convenient corner. When cleaning up, always keep a piece of wet paper on top of the others. Every time he wants to "squat," he will seek out this spot and use the papers. (This routine is rarely necessary for more than three days.) Now leave your Bichon puppy for the night. Quite probably he will cry and howl a bit; some are more stubborn than others on this matter. But let him stay alone for the night. This may seem harsh treatment, but it is the best procedure in the long run. Just let him cry; he will weary of it sooner or later.

Going to a new home can be quite intimidating for a small puppy like the Bichon. Handle him gently and give him lots of love and care to help him feel at ease.

TRAINING YOUR BICHON

You owe proper training to your Bichon. The right and privilege of being trained is his birthright; and whether your Bichon is going to be a handsome, well-mannered housedog and companion, a show dog, or whatever possible use he may be put to, the basic training is always the same—all must start with basic obedience, or what might be called "manner training."

Your Bichon must come instantly when called and obey the "Sit" or "Down" command just as fast; he must walk quietly at "Heel," whether on or off lead. He must be mannerly and polite wherever he goes; he must be polite to strangers on the street and in stores. He must be mannerly in the presence of other dogs. He must not bark at children on roller skates, motorcycles, or other domestic animals. And he must be restrained from chasing cats. It is not a dog's inalienable right to chase cats, and he must be reprimanded for it.

Whether you select an adult or a puppy, a show dog or a house pet, all Bichons need to be trained properly.

PROFESSIONAL TRAINING

How do you go about this training? Well, it's a very simple procedure, pretty well standardized by now. First, if you can afford the extra expense, you

The highly trainable Bichon is capable of learning to do almost anything. However, when it comes to driving, that's probably best left to the owner!

may send your Bichon to a professional trainer, where in 30 to 60 days he will learn how to be a "good dog." If you enlist the services of a good professional trainer, follow his advice of when to come to see the dog. No, he won't forget you, but too-frequent visits at the wrong time may slow down his training progress. And using a "pro" trainer means that you will have to go for some training, too, after the trainer feels your Bichon is ready to go home. You will have to learn how your Bichon works, just what to expect of him and how to use what the dog has learned after he is home.

OBEDIENCE TRAINING CLASS

Another way to train your Bichon (many experienced Bichon people think this is the best) is to join an obedience training class right in your own community. There is such a group in nearly every community nowadays. Here you will be working with a group of people who are also just starting out. You will actually be training your own dog, since all work is done under the direction of a head trainer who will make suggestions to you and also tell you when and how to correct your Bichon's errors. Then, too, working with such a group, your Bichon will learn to get along with other dogs. And, what is more important, he will learn to do exactly what he is told to do, no matter how much confusion there is around him or how great the temptation is to go his own way.

Write to your national kennel club for the location of a training club or class in your locality. Sign up. Go to it regularly—every session! Go early and leave late! Both you and your Bichon will benefit tremendously.

TRAIN HIM BY THE BOOK

The third way of training your Bichon is by the book. Yes, you can do it this way and do a good job of it too. But in using the book method, select a book, buy it, study it carefully; then study it some more, until the procedures are almost second nature to you. Then start your training. But stay with the book and its advice and exercises. Don't start in and then make up a few rules of your own. If you don't follow the book, you'll get into jams you can't get out of by yourself. If after a few hours of short training sessions your Bichon is still not working as he should, get back to the book for a study session, because it's your fault, not the dog's! The procedures of dog training have been so well systemized that it must be your fault, since literally thousands of fine Bichons have been trained by the book.

After your Bichon is "letter perfect" under all conditions, then, if you wish, go on to advanced training and trick work.

Your Bichon will love his obedience training, and you'll burst with pride at the finished product! Your Bichon will enjoy life even more, and you'll enjoy your Bichon more. And remember—you *owe good training to your Bichon.*

Successful Dog Training **is one of the better books by which you can train your Bichon. It is written by Hollywood dog trainer Michael Kamer.**

FEEDING YOUR BICHON

Now let's talk about feeding your Bichon, a subject so simple that it's amazing there is so much nonsense and misunderstanding about it. Is it expensive to feed a Bichon? No, it is not! You can feed your Bichon economically and keep him in perfect shape the year round, or you can feed him expensively. He'll thrive either way, and let's see why this is true.

First of all, remember a Bichon is a dog. Dogs do not have a high degree of selectivity in their food, and unless you spoil them with great variety (and possibly turn them into poor, "picky" eaters) they will eat almost anything that they become accustomed to. Many dogs flatly refuse to eat nice, fresh beef. They pick around it and eat everything else. But meat—bah! Why? They aren't accustomed to it! They'd eat rabbit fast enough, but they refuse beef because they aren't used to it.

VARIETY NOT NECESSARY

A good general rule of thumb is forget all human preferences and don't give a thought to variety. Choose the right diet for your Bichon and feed it to him day after day, year after year, winter and summer. But what is the right diet?

Variety is not a necessary part of a healthy dog's diet. Choose a nutritionally balanced food for your Bichon and feed it to him every day.

Hundreds of thousands of dollars have been spent in canine nutrition research. The results are pretty conclusive, so you needn't go into a lot of experimenting with trials of this and that every other week. Research has proven just what your dog needs to eat and to keep healthy.

DOG FOOD

There are almost as many right diets as there are dog experts, but the basic diet most often recommended is one that consists of a dry food, either meal or kibble form. There are several of excellent quality, manufactured by reliable companies, research tested, and nationally advertised. They are inexpensive, highly satisfactory, and easily available in stores everywhere in containers of five to 50 pounds. Larger amounts cost less per pound, usually.

If you have a choice of brands, it is usually safer to choose the better known one; but even so, carefully read the analysis on the package. Do not choose any food in which the protein level is less than 25 percent, and be sure that this protein comes from both animal and vegetable sources. The good dog foods have meat meal, fish meal, liver, and such, plus protein from alfalfa and soy beans, as well as some dried-milk product. Note the vitamin content carefully. See that they are all there in good proportions; and be especially certain that the food contains properly high levels of vitamins A and D, two of the most perishable and important ones.

An ideal snack for the Bichon is the Chicken Chooz™. It is a hard molded bone of chicken and cheese that satisfies the dog's appetite and chewing needs. This is a very high-quality and high-protein product with 70% protein content.

Note the B-complex level, but don't worry about carbohydrate and mineral levels. These substances are plentiful and cheap and not likely to be lacking in a good brand.

The advice given for how to choose a dry food also applies to moist or canned types of dog foods, if you decide to feed one of these.

Having chosen a really good food, feed it to your Bichon as the manufacturer directs. And once you've started, stick to it. Never change if you can possibly help it. A switch from one meal or kibble-type food can usually be made without too much upset; however, a change will almost invariably give you (and your Bichon) some trouble.

puppies. Vitamins and minerals are naturally present in all the foods; and to ensure against any loss through processing, they are added in concentrated form to the dog food you use. Except on the advice of your veterinarian, added amounts of vitamins can prove harmful to your Bichon! The same risk goes with minerals.

Start a feeding schedule for your Bichon and stick to it. These puppies know when it's time to eat and they come running at meal time!

WHEN SUPPLEMENTS ARE NEEDED

Now what about supplements of various kinds, mineral and vitamin, or the various oils? They are all okay to add to your Bichon's food. However, if you are feeding your Bichon a correct diet, and this is easy to do, no supplements are necessary unless your Bichon has been improperly fed, has been sick, or is having

FEEDING SCHEDULE

When and how much food to give your Bichon? Most dogs do better if fed two or three smaller meals per day—this is not only better but vital to larger and deep-chested dogs. As to how to prepare the food and how much to give, it is generally best to follow the directions on the food package. Your own Bichon may want a little more or a little less.

Fresh, cool water should always be available to your Bichon. This is important to good health throughout his lifetime.

ALL BICHONS NEED TO CHEW

Puppies and young Bichons need something with resistance to chew on while their teeth and jaws are developing—for cutting the puppy teeth, to induce growth of the permanent teeth under the puppy teeth, to assist in getting rid of the puppy teeth at the proper time, to help the permanent teeth through the gums, to ensure normal jaw development, and to settle the permanent teeth solidly in the jaws.

The adult Bichon's desire to chew stems from the instinct for tooth cleaning, gum massage, and jaw exercise—plus the need for an outlet for periodic doggie tensions.

Bichon puppies love to chew! The raised dental tips on the Plaque Attackers™ chew devices help to clean your Bichon's teeth and massage his gums as he chews.

Nylabones® not only keep your Bichon's teeth clean but they also provide an excellent source of entertainment and relief from "doggie tensions."

This is why dogs, especially puppies and young dogs, will often destroy property worth hundreds of dollars when their chewing instinct is not diverted from their owner's possessions. And this is why you should provide your Bichon with something to chew—something that has the necessary functional qualities, is desirable from the Bichon's viewpoint, and is safe for him.

It is very important that your Bichon not be permitted to chew on anything he can break or on any indigestible thing from which he can bite sizable chunks. Sharp pieces, such as from a bone which can be broken by a dog, may pierce the intestinal wall and kill.

Pet shops sell real bones that have been colored, cooked, dyed, or served natural. Some of these bones are too large for Bichons.

Indigestible things that can be bitten off in chunks, such as from shoes or rubber or plastic toys, may cause an intestinal stoppage (if not regurgitated) and bring painful death, unless surgery is promptly performed.

Strong natural bones, such as 4- to 8-inch lengths of round shin bone from mature beef—either the kind you can get from a butcher or one of the variety available commercially in pet stores—may serve your Bichon's teething needs if his mouth is large enough to handle them effectively. You may be tempted to give your Bichon puppy a smaller bone and he may not be able to break it when you do, but puppies grow rapidly and the power of their jaws constantly increases until maturity. This means that a growing Bichon may break one of the smaller bones at any time, swallow the pieces, and die painfully before you realize what is wrong.

All hard natural bones are very abrasive. If your Bichon is an avid chewer, natural bones may wear away his teeth prematurely; hence, they then should be taken away from your dog when the teething purposes have been served. The badly worn, and usually painful, teeth of many mature dogs can be traced to excessive chewing on natural bones.

Contrary to popular belief, knuckle bones that can be chewed up and swallowed by your

Raised dental tips on each dog bone work wonders with controlling plaque on a Bichon's teeth. Get a medium-sized (regular) Nylabone® for your Bichon.

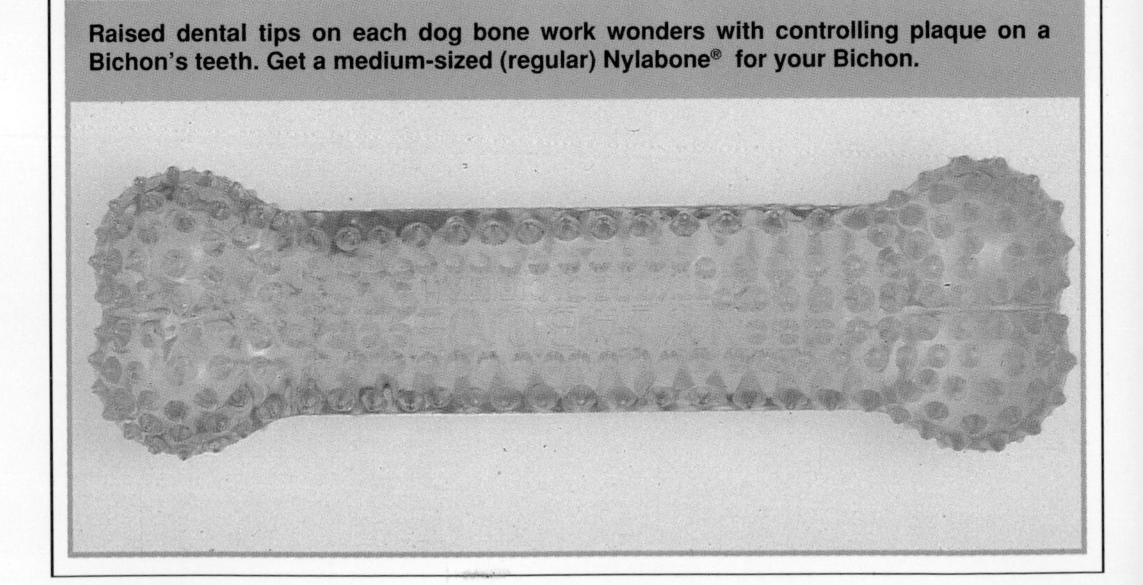

Bichon provide little, if any, usable calcium or other nutriment. They do, however, disturb the digestion of most dogs and cause them to vomit the nourishing food they need.

Dried rawhide products of various types, shapes, sizes, and prices are available on the market and have become quite popular. However, they don't serve the primary chewing functions very well; they are a bit messy when wet from mouthing, and most Bichons chew them up rather rapidly—but they have been considered safe for dogs until recently. Now, more and more incidents of death, and near death, by strangulation have been reported to be the results of partially swallowed chunks of rawhide swelling in the throat. More recently, some veterinarians have been attributing cases of acute constipation to large pieces of incompletely digested rawhide in the intestine.

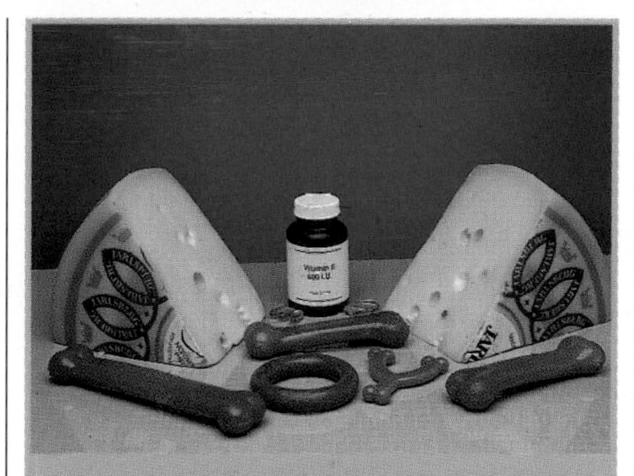

Pet shops sell dog treats that are healthy and nutritious. Cheese is added to chicken meal and other high protein ingredients to be molded into hard chew devices. If the pacifier doesn't have at least a 50% protein content, keep looking!

A new product, molded rawhide, is very safe. During the process, the rawhide is melted and then injection molded into the familiar dog shape. It is very hard and is eagerly accepted by Bichons. The melting process also

Molded rawhide called Roar-Hide™ by Nylabone® is very hard and safe for your dog. It is eagerly accepted by Bichons.

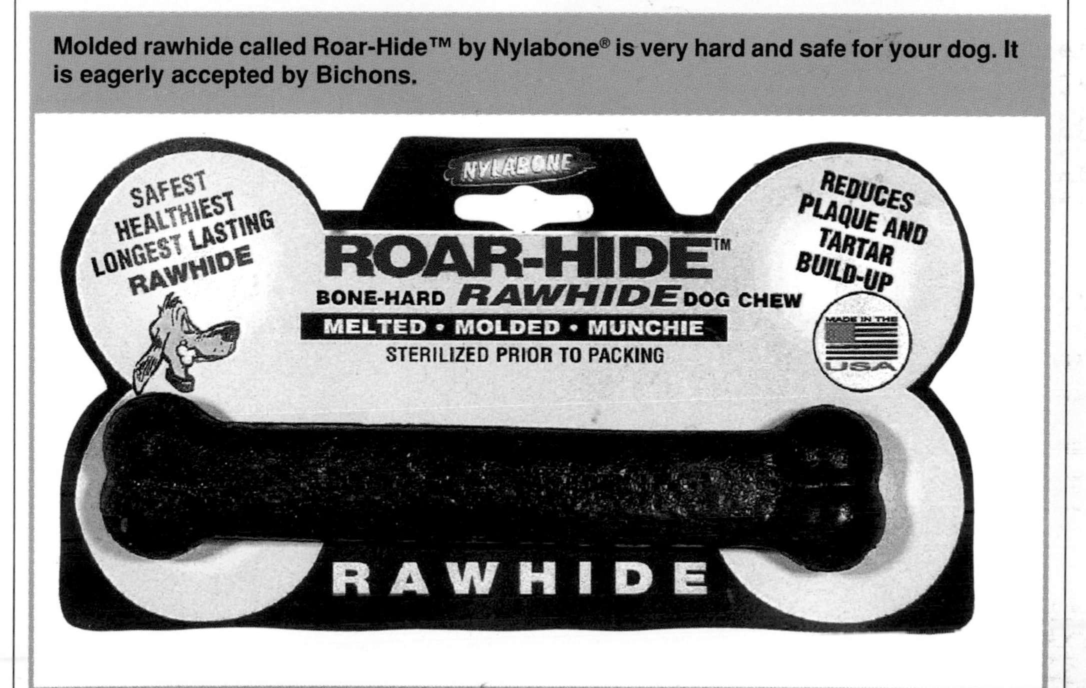

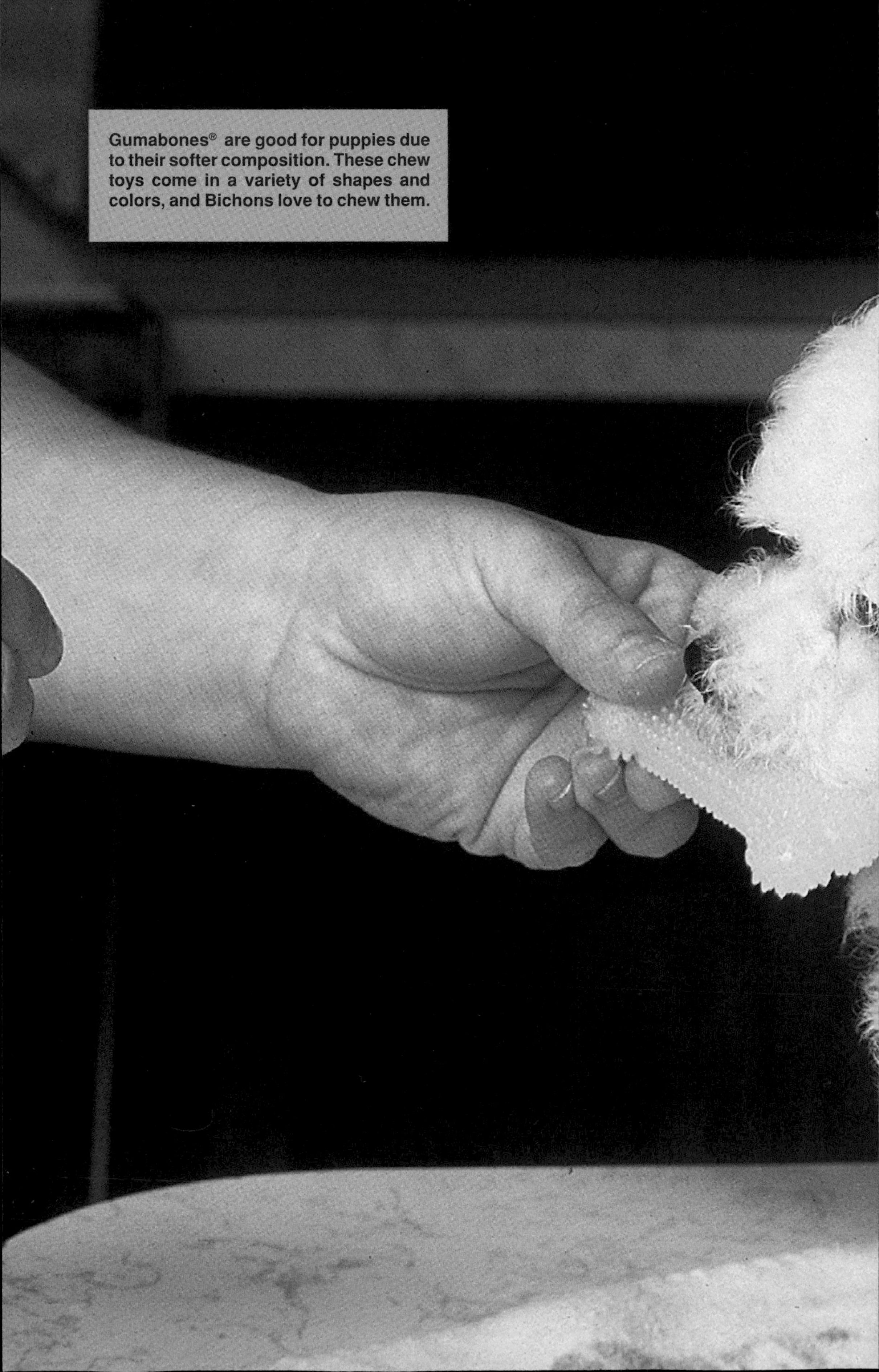

Gumabones® are good for puppies due to their softer composition. These chew toys come in a variety of shapes and colors, and Bichons love to chew them.

sterilizes the rawhide. Don't confuse this with pressed rawhide, which is nothing more than small strips of rawhide squeezed together.

A chicken-flavored Gumabone® has tiny particles of chicken embedded in it to keep the Bichon interested in chewing it. Bichons can smell it but you can't—that's the way it should be!

The nylon bones, especially those with natural meat and bone fractions added, are probably the most complete, safe, and economical answer to the chewing need. Dogs cannot break them or bite off sizable chunks; hence, they are completely safe—and being longer lasting than other things offered for the purpose, they are economical.

Hard chewing raises little bristle-like projections on the surface of the nylon bones—to provide effective interim tooth cleaning and vigorous gum massage, much in the same way your toothbrush does it for you. The little projections are raked off and swallowed in the form of thin shavings, but the chemistry of the nylon is such that they break down in the stomach fluids and pass through without effect.

The toughness of the nylon provides the strong chewing resistance needed for important jaw exercise and effectively aids teething functions, but there is no tooth wear because nylon is non-abrasive. Being inert, nylon does not support the growth of microorganisms; and it can be washed in soap and water or it can be sterilized by boiling or in an autoclave.

Nylabone® is highly recommended by veterinarians as a safe, healthy nylon bone that can't splinter or chip. Nylabone® is

There are special bones made just for puppies. They are usually filled with calcium supplements and are very hard. The most popular of the puppy bones is the one made by Nylabone®.

The Gumabone® Frisbee™ has a dog bone molded on top to make it easier for the dog to pick up. It's a durable chew toy that also provides fun and exercise for your Bichon. *The trademark Frisbee™ is used under license from Mattel, Inc., California, USA.

frizzled by the dog's chewing action, creating a toothbrush-like surface that cleanses the teeth and massages the gums. Nylabone®, the only chew products made of flavor-impregnated solid nylon, are available in your local pet shop. Nylabone® is superior to the cheaper bones because it is made of virgin nylon, which is the strongest and longest-lasting type of nylon available. The cheaper bones are made from recycled or re-ground nylon scraps, and have a tendency to break apart and split easily.

Nothing, however, substitutes for periodic professional attention for your Bichon's teeth and gums, not any more than your toothbrush can do that for you. Have your Bichon's teeth cleaned at least once a year by your veterinarian (twice a year is better) and he will be happier, healthier, and far more pleasant to live with.

GROOMING YOUR BICHON

The Bichon Frise is a white double-coated dog that requires more grooming care than most breeds. The coat requires constant brushing and combing. Puppies have a soft single coat that gradually begins to develop coarser guard hairs at about one year of age. The full luxurious coat of the Bichon begins to take shape with proper grooming at about two years of age. Some coats don't reach maturity until three years of age. While the Bichon completes a good percentage of its growth by the age of eight to nine months, and full growth and "medical" maturity between one year and eighteen months, the maturation process can continue until as much as three years of age. While height and weight may remain essentially the same, anatomical features considered significant according to the standard may continue to get better or worse. In this sense, the Bichon is a "late bloomer." This is especially true in the case of coat. Many Bichons whose coats are disappointing late in puppyhood, or even as late as two years of age, may achieve beautiful coats by age three or even later with proper care and diet. The Bichon's general health is directly related, of course, to the quality of the coat. Adequate and balanced nutrition is absolutely necessary for a good coat.

The Bichon's white double coat requires constant brushing and combing to prevent matting and to maintain the desired "powder puff" appearance.

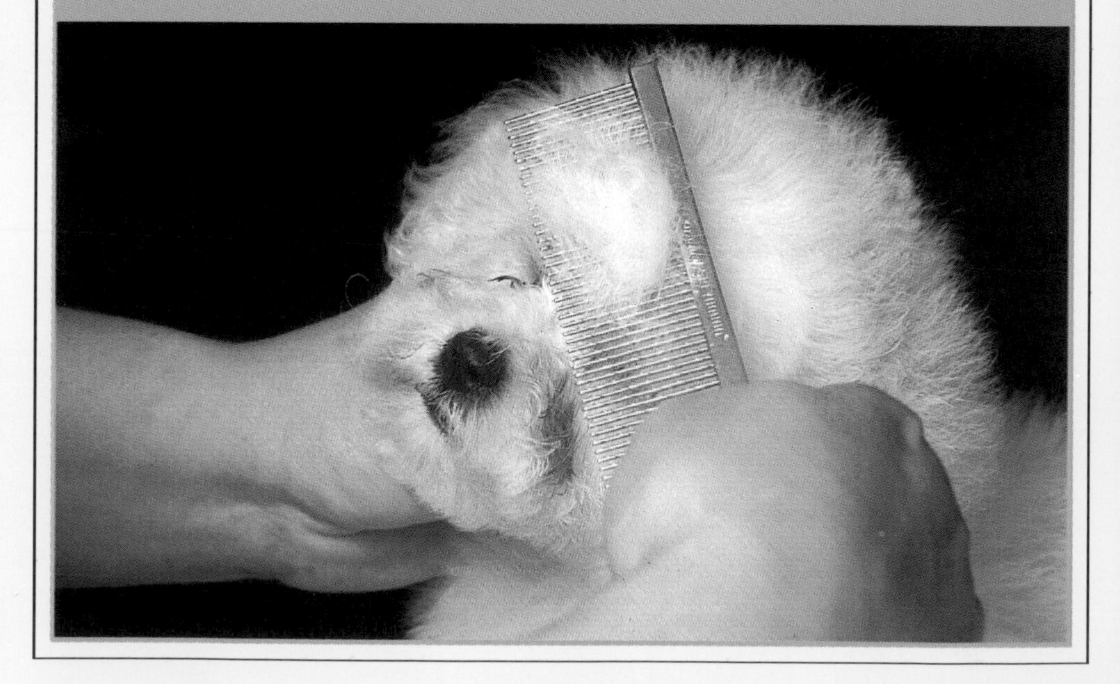

Bichons require frequent bathing, more than what is needed for many other breeds. A Bichon puppy who is introduced to bathing at a young age will quickly become accustomed to the routine.

Aggressive breeding for coat, especially in the US, has improved the general quality of Bichon coats world-wide. The attention given to coat and grooming at US shows has attracted world-wide attention and has helped propel the breed forward to prominence. Through the years, a Bichon Frise show cut has evolved in harmony with the US standard's attempts to emphasize the specifics through detailed description. The "outline" or overall look of the coat should make the dog look as close to the standard as possible. A well-outlined dog will be cut in a way that enhances its movement and allows it to seem to glide effortlessly in a way matched by few, if any, breeds.

Bichons need to be bathed frequently, more than most breeds, and proper coat care requires careful drying. Fleas and ticks are an especially serious problem with double-coated breeds, and flea infestation can destroy a beautiful coat in no time. Many Bichon owners find it far easier and more cost effective in the long run to have grooming done professionally by groomers who "know" the breed. In this regard, the Bichon, as with other double-coated breeds, is not for everyone and may be inappropriate for those without the means or inclination to properly groom their dogs.

In a show cut, the Bichon's body hair is trimmed to enhance the outline of the dog and compliment his movement. The facial furnishings and head hair are left longer and trimmed to give a rounded look.

YOUR BICHON'S HEALTH

The Bichon Frise, the updated version of the Tenerife dog known as the Bichon à Poil Frisé, is generally, with proper breeding, a very healthy breed. This was, along with his appearance, one of the reasons for his early popularity. There are no particular problems peculiar to the Bichon Frise in old age, which is fortunate because they live so long. This is a further indication that the Bichon is a naturally occurring breed.

A HEALTHY DIET

A proper well-balanced diet is a must for the Bichon Frise. Feeding a high-quality puppy food and, in due course, a dog food supplemented with proteins, such as chicken, turkey, and beef, is an excellent regimen. Well-cooked vegetables are also a good addition with most dogs. Rice may work wonders along with cooked chopped meat when the Bichon has gastrointestinal distress. Some Bichons, as well as all other breeds, can develop food allergies to almost anything. Some cannot tolerate the beet pulp found in many dog foods, even premium ones. It is sometimes wise to put the allergic Bichon on a lamb and rice formula. There are digestive aids, such as enzyme enhancers, to ease digestion and improve coat.

A healthy diet is essential for a healthy Bichon. It is important to always feed your Bichon puppy a high-quality, nutritionally balanced puppy food.

VACCINATIONS

Throughout the Bichon's lifetime, which can last as long as 20 years (17 and 18 years are commonplace), you will have to make certain that he is vaccinated against certain canine diseases. These include distemper, hepatitis, leptospirosis, parvovirus, bordetella or kennel cough, coronavirus, and parainfluenza.

After completing his puppy series, your Bichon will have to be revaccinated every year. Puppies usually receive their first shots before they leave the breeder at approximately six weeks of age. Your veterinarian will then schedule follow-up vaccinations at the 8–10 week mark and then again at 12 weeks.

The most common shot is the "five-in-one" shot, which includes distemper, hepatitis, leptospirosis, bordetella, and parvovirus. There have been reported cases (only a tiny percentage of the inoculated canine population) of severe reactions and sometimes permanent neurological impairment, including partial paralysis, resulting from the "five-in-one" shot. This has prompted many Bichon owners to insist that the parvo vaccine be given separately from the others after a safe interval. Further, there have been reports of rare cases in which pets have contracted parvo or suffered severe reaction to the "live" parvo vaccine. An alternative is the "killed" parvo vaccine, which requires several more inoculations over a longer period of time and more frequent boosters. Both of these phenomena are emphatically denied by the drug companies that produce the "live" parvo and "five-in-one" vaccines, claiming that there is no proven scientific basis for establishing a cause and effect relationship between their products and the reported cases

Your Bichon puppy will probably receive his first vaccinations before you bring him home. Your veterinarian will set up a schedule for follow-up shots and annual boosters.

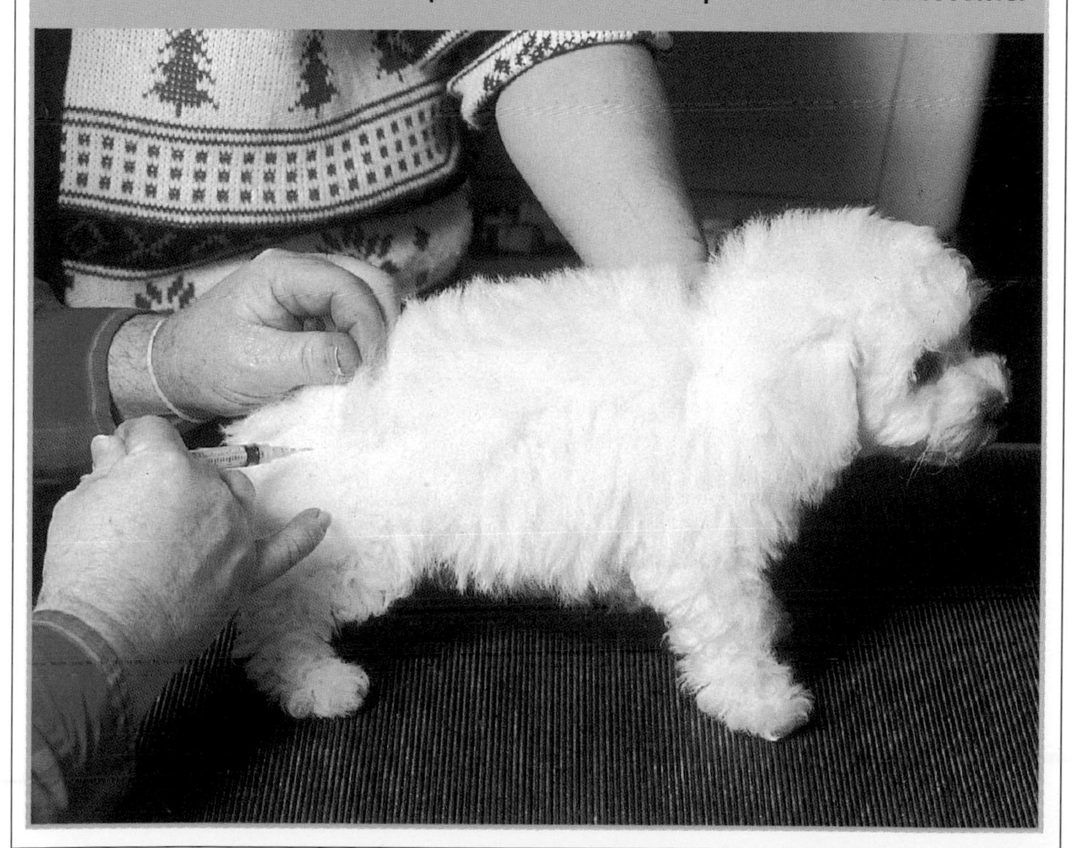

of side effects. Nevertheless, whatever the merits of the respective claims and counter-claims, responsible Bichon Frise owners may wish to avoid taking any chances and stay on the side of caution by using the "killed" parvo vaccination separate from the other vaccinations.

Regional differences can dictate changes in the required vaccinations and their sequences. One of the most important shots and one that is required by law is the rabies inoculation. Because of mass inoculation programs, rabies is all but extinct in some parts of the world, such as England. It is still a problem in the US where there is a larger wild animal population. The Bichon Frise is not a large, roaming, field animal and the chance of contact with a rabid raccoon, fox, or other animal is minimal. Nevertheless, all Bichons, as well as all other breeds, should be vaccinated as pups against rabies and receive their annual booster shots.

Another problem related to region and climate is heartworm. Bichons in the states with sub-tropical climates, such as Florida and southern California, should be kept on daily or monthly anti-heartworm programs all year round. Those in more temperate or northerly climates should be on a program in the warmer months, especially during the mosquito season. All breeds, including the Bichon, should be checked annually by blood test for heartworm infestation, even when continuously kept on an anti-heartworm preventive formula.

PARASITES

The great enemy of coat and skin are external parasites such as ticks, lice, and fleas. Strict and uncompromising control in the all-around war against fleas is absolutely necessary. The total environment must be attacked in an aggressive way to prevent parasite infestation. One adult female flea can lay many hundreds of eggs that will hatch and become adults in less than three weeks.

Good veterinary care for your Bichon includes regular dental check ups and cleanings to remove any plaque that may have accumulated. A Bichon owner can take an active part in maintaininghis dog's dental health at home.

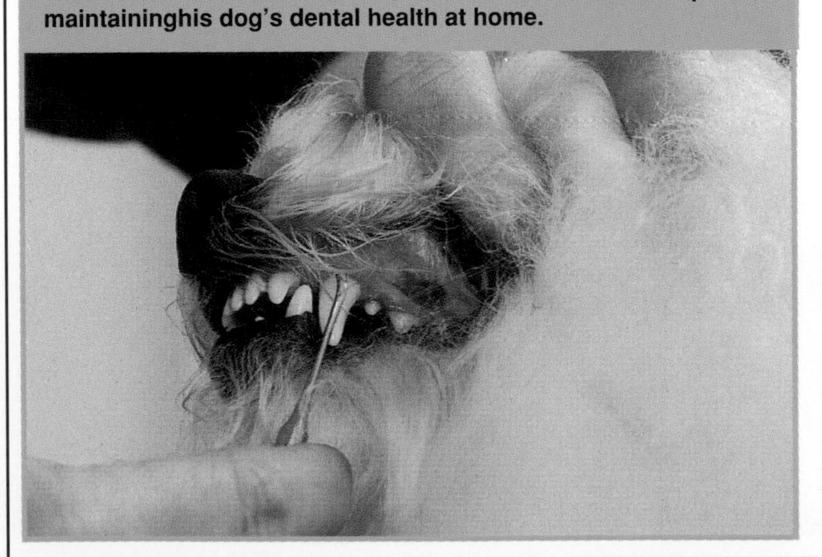

Although your Bichon may not believe it, Nylafloss® is not a toy but rather a most effective agent in removing destructive plaque between teeth and beneath the gumline. Gentle tugging is all that is needed to activate Nylafloss®.

Fleas brought into the house by the pet get into the carpets and begin to multiply. Since the fleas feed on your pet's blood, a severe infestation can cause anemia in the animal.

Ticks, which are found in wooded areas and fields, can attach themselves to an animal. There are many types of ticks, including the deer tick that carries Lyme disease. If you live in a wooded area, always check your pet for ticks and also have it vaccinated against Lyme disease.

DENTAL PROBLEMS

Small dogs such as the Bichon Frise are especially prone to periodontal disease, which causes bone recession and tooth loss as well as bacterial infection. Good veterinary care should include regular dental check ups and periodic cleaning to remove plaque that can build up under the gum line. In some cases requiring periodontal work, a canine dentist may be necessary, although this should be unnecessary if the owner provides proper dental care, including brushing, on a regular basis. Dogs in the wild keep their teeth clean by chewing bones and hard foods that normally are not part of the domestic Bichon's diet. Hard dry food along with some safe commercially available chew toys, such as the products made by

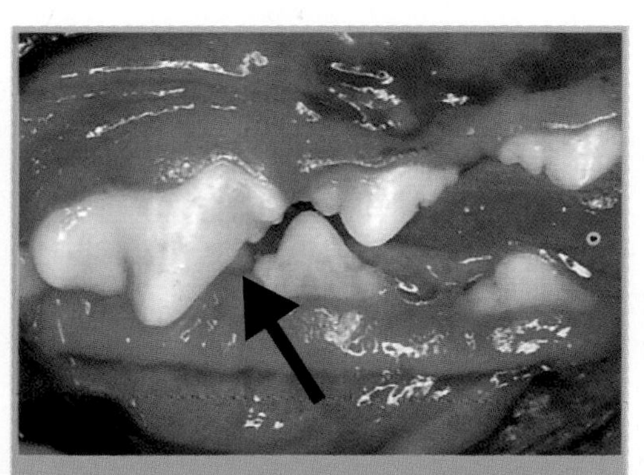

ABOVE: This scientific study shows a dog's tooth (arrow) while being maintained by Gumabone® chewing. BELOW: The Gumabone® was taken away and in 30 days the tooth was almost completely covered with plaque and tartar.

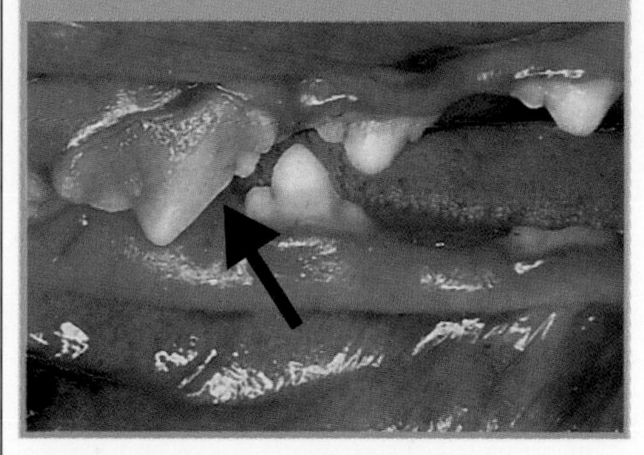

Nylabone®, can help prevent the buildup of plaque. The Bichon's teeth should be brushed frequently by his owner, at least a few times a week. With proper training and gentle persuasion, the little guy should learn to tolerate having his teeth brushed

When selecting a Bichon—or any other small dog, like the Poodle—be certain that breeders are screening for weak stifles and other problems that may hinder your pet's movement.

and allow you full access to his mouth.

SPECIFIC HEALTH PROBLEMS SEEN IN THE BICHON

As with other breeds, popularity is not without its price. Despite the dedication and Herculean efforts of the early American breeders and the various Bichon Frise clubs and organizations, the success of the beautiful coiffed little dog in the show ring has had some inevitable consequences. To meet the increased demand, some unscrupulous breeders and some who are just plain incompetent have engaged in large scale mass production of puppies. Indiscriminate breeding and much repetitive inbreeding has occurred. Serious defects that should have been controlled have been glossed over and buried in sloppy breeding programs. Not the least of these have been dental problems, including sensitive gums, overbites, and an increase in periodontal disorders.

Weakness in Stifles

In recent years, several breeding lines have been deeply troubled by a high incidence of weakness in the stifles or kneecaps. The condition is known as medial patellar luxation, and it involves the dislocation of the kneecap(s). This is a direct result of bad breeding. It is a condition that can be controlled through careful, selective breeding and intelligent genetic engineering but unfortunately has been creeping its way into the Bichon population. It is a condition that interferes with the natural gait of the Bichon and, of course, prevents good, sound movement. In extreme cases, it can partially disable the dog and is considered a severe defect.

Eye Disorders

Some bloodlines have been plagued with juvenile cataracts or the onset of cataracts at a very young age. This disorder, normally associated with older dogs, can affect even puppies. There have been reports of a case in which a puppy was blinded by cataracts at eight months of age. This disorder is almost entirely a genetic phenomenon and a direct result of careless breeding or crossbreeding motivated by profit. No dog with this malady in its breeding line should be bred, even if there have been no cases for a few generations.

Bladder Stones

Small breeds are generally prone to bladder stones, which are uncommon in most larger breeds. Bladder stones are frequently the result of too much protein, magnesium, or phosphorus in the dog's diet. The symptoms of bladder stones are varied and if left untreated can cause urinary blockage and serious kidney damage. Occasionally, bladder stones need to be surgically removed, but the most common treatment is dietary adjustment and management beginning with a drastic reduction in protein consumption. The special diets strictly control the mineral content of the dog's food. These minerals tend to form crystals in the dog's bladder. This is especially true if the dog has been left for long periods between walks and the bladder is infrequently evacuated. Waste products in combination with the minerals have the potential to crystallize and form stones. It is best said that the stones are a combination of heredity, diet, lifestyle or environment, and daily habits. Even if your Bichon has the genetic potential for bladder stones, you may never know it if you walk him frequently and give him a healthy lifestyle complete with a lot of exercise and a sensible diet.

It is sometimes best to stop feeding your Bichon high protein puppy foods at about eight

The undisputed champion of dog health books is Dr. Lowell Ackerman's encyclopedic work *Owner's Guide to Dog Health*. It covers everything that dog owners may need to know about. It is actually a complete veterinarian's handbook in easy-to-understand language.

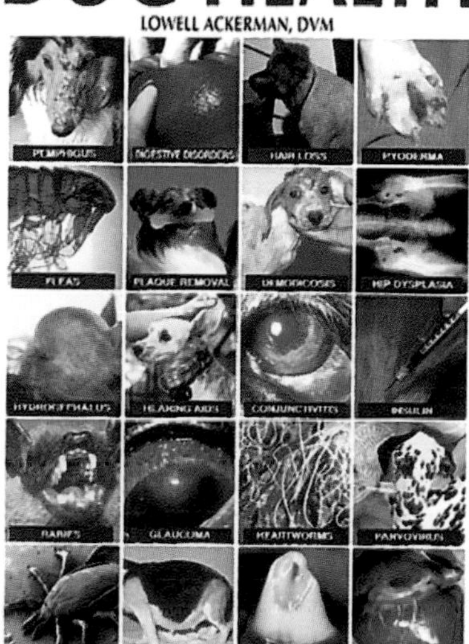

months of age when he has largely achieved full growth, although he doesn't reach maturity until between one and one and a half years of age. An adult dog food that is slightly lower in protein or a food that has a moderate protein level might be desirable. This is especially true if you notice excessive urination, an early symptom of bladder stones. If you have any reason to suspect bladder stones in your Bichon, do not hesitate to consult your veterinarian, as delay can be serious or even fatal. In addition to straining or difficulty in passing urine, a general malaise, or weakness, including disinterest in food, may indicate the presence of stones.

Hip Dysplasia

According to medical authority, hip dysplasia is all but nonexistent in the Bichon Frise. Historically, the little Tenerife was practically free of this deformity, which can have crippling effects and shorten a dog's life. However rare, it does exist and is a most certainly a product of increased breeding activity. Even when present in Bichons, the dog's small size allows the condition to be tolerated with less of a disabling effect than in larger dogs with larger legs and bigger strides. Conversely, the absence of any apparent deformity, discomfort, or discernible movement problem does not in itself rule out hip dysplasia.

Hip dysplasia is rare in the Bichon, but it is not nonexistent. Small breeds like the Bichon, however, are able to tolerate this condition better than larger, longer-legged breeds.

Epilepsy

The canine medical community now recognizes that overbreeding has caused epilepsy in some Bichon bloodlines. Happily, it is still rather rare, although epilepsy occurs more frequently in Bichons than in larger breeds. It exists in the breed in its petit mal and grand mal forms. Epilepsy, when it occurs, is of the adult onset type, meaning that it occurs in mature adult dogs. It can be successfully controlled with medication as prescribed by your veterinarian.

Poor Pigmentation

A rare hereditary defect found in the Bichon Frise is poor pigmentation. The Bichon's skin pigmentation is preferably dark—the nose, lips, and eye rims are universally required by breed standards to be dark or black. Pale, weak, or spotted pigmentation of these body parts is considered a defect, but not an indication of other skin problems.

Heredity and indiscriminate breeding practices are two major contributors to the perpetuation of health problems in some Bichon bloodlines.

Allergies

Generally, the Bichon Frise has few skin allergies or skin problems if properly groomed. Proper grooming is a must and should be considered a part of the Bichon's general health care. Grooming has an important place in the remarkable popularity and evolution of the breed. The changes brought about have, like most things, been both good and bad. With the larger fuller coats of today's Bichons, the need for good grooming as a health measure assumes paramount importance. Their fine hair tends to mat, which can cause multiple skin problems when the dirt in the matted hair is held tightly to the skin. Skin problems caused by contact irritants, not by allergies, are not problems associated with the Bichon.

Under/Overshot Bite

While not a medical problem, an unusually undershot or overshot bite is a defect often associated with indiscriminate breeding practices. Aggressive dental care is a must for this breed. Like some other small breeds, Bichons have a strong tendency toward heavy tartar and plaque formation that, if left to accumulate, leads to tooth loss and eventually to bacteria that can cause damage to vital organs when transmitted through the bloodstream.

Temperament

Probably the greatest problem associated with overbreeding is unstable temperament. The Bichon Frise is a playful happy little dog. He is sensitive and gay with a most cheerful attitude. He is friendly, outgoing, and very lively, as well as stable of disposition. All of these are accurate time-honored descriptions of the Bichon Frise as he has been known to many generations, even when he was called by other names. The Bichon's wonderful temperament is a major reason for his fantastic rise from obscurity to celebrity. His temperament, which was the very quality (along with the full-coated look) that catapulted him into world-wide popularity, also created a large demand for puppies. This caused the excessive, irresponsible breeding activities that began in order to meet the demand, which in turn had ill effects on the breed, including temperament problems. Bad breeding is the number one cause, and may be just about the only cause save severe environmental deprivation, for behavior problems in the Bichon Frise. Nervousness and high anxiety when left alone are likely symptoms of genetic change.

The Bichon Frise, by and large, is still unspoiled. Nevertheless, a small percentage of Bichons now have temperament problems of one type or another. Despite what has been written about the "new" problems created by large-scale breeding, the Bichon is still largely unchanged and the defects described occur in only a small minority of cases. He is still the same hardy happy little dog with a splendid temperament. He is good with children and other pets, even cats, and he loves company—both human and animal.

Good temperament runs in the family! The friendly faces of this adult and puppy Bichon show the wonderful disposition that helped catapult the breed into worldwide popularity.

Conscientious breeding by reputable breeders helps to produce healthy, stable Bichon puppies. Just look at this bright-eyed bunch of Bichon babies!

SHOWING YOUR BICHON

A show Bichon is a comparatively rare thing. He is one out of several litters of puppies. He happens to be born with a degree of physical perfection that closely approximates the standard by which the breed is judged in the show ring. Such a dog should, on maturity, be able to win or approach his championship in good, fast company at the larger shows. Upon finishing his championship, he is apt to be as highly desirable as a breeding animal. As a proven stud, he will automatically command a high price for service.

Showing Bichons is a lot of fun—yes, but it is a highly competitive sport. While all the experts were once beginners, the odds are against a novice. You will be showing against experienced handlers, often people who have devoted a lifetime to breeding, picking the right ones, and then showing those dogs through to their championships. Moreover, the most perfect Bichon ever born has faults, and in your hands the faults will be far more evident than with the experienced handler who knows how to minimize his Bichon's faults. These are but a few points on the sad side of the picture.

Earning a conformation championship is no easy task for the Bichon, considering that competition on every level is very intense.

A handler gets her Bichon ready to be examined by the conformation judge.

The experienced handler, as I say, was not born knowing the ropes. He learned—*and so can you!* You can if you will put in the same time, study and keen observation that he did. But it will take time!

KEY TO SUCCESS

First, search for a truly fine show prospect. Take the puppy home, raise him by the book, and as carefully as you know how, give him every chance to mature into the Bichon you hoped for. My

"Heel" is an important command that every Bichon needs to know. It is necessary for the show dog, as he will have to demonstrate heeling with his handler in the show ring.

advice is to keep your dog out of big shows, even Puppy Classes, until he is mature. Maturity in the male is roughly two years; with the female, 14 months or so. When your Bichon is approaching maturity, start out at match shows, and, with this experience for both of you, then go gunning for the big wins at the big shows.

The distinctive gait of the Bichon is something to watch! This Bichon holds his head high as he prances and shows off his proud strut.

Next step, read the standard by which the Bichon is judged. Study it until you know it by heart. Having done this, and while your puppy is at home (where he should be) growing into a normal, healthy Bichon, go to every dog show you can possibly reach. Sit at the ringside and watch Bichon judging. Keep your ears and eyes open. Do your own judging, holding each of those dogs against the standard, which you now know by heart.

In your evaluations, don't start looking for faults. Look for the virtues—the best qualities. How does a given Bichon shape up against the standard? Having looked for and noted the virtues, then note the faults and see what prevents a given Bichon from standing correctly or moving well. Weigh these faults against the virtues, since, ideally, every feature of the dog should contribute to the harmonious whole dog.

"RINGSIDE JUDGING"

It's a good practice to make notes on each Bichon, always holding the dog against the standard. In "ringside judging," forget your personal preference for this or that feature. What does the standard say about it? Watch carefully as the judge places the dogs in a given class. It is difficult from the ringside always to see why number one was placed over the second dog. Try to follow the judge's reasoning. Later try to talk with the judge after he is finished. Ask him questions as to why he placed certain Bichons and not others. Listen while the judge explains his placings, and, I'll say right here, any judge worthy of his license should be able to give reasons.

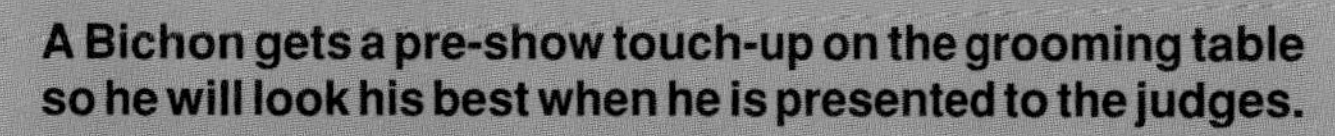

A Bichon gets a pre-show touch-up on the grooming table so he will look his best when he is presented to the judges.

A show Bichon must be groomed to perfection. The Bichon's coat takes a lot of work to maintain and trim in order to achieve the desired "look."

When you're not at the ringside, talk with the fanciers and breeders who have Bichons. Don't be afraid to ask opinions or say that you don't know. You have a lot of listening to do, and it will help you a great deal and speed up your personal progress if you are a good listener.

THE NATIONAL CLUB

You will find it worthwhile to join the national Bichon club and to subscribe to its magazine.

From the national club, you will learn the location of an approved regional club near you. Now, when your young Bichon is eight to ten months old, find out the dates of match shows in your section of the country. These differ from regular shows only in that no championship points are given. These shows are especially designed to launch young dogs (and new handlers) on a show career.

ENTER MATCH SHOWS

With the ring deportment you have watched at big shows firmly in mind and practice, enter your Bichon in as many match shows as you can. When in the ring, you have two jobs. One is to see to it that your Bichon is always being seen to its best advantage. The other job is to keep your eye on the judge to see what he may want you to do next. Watch only the judge and your Bichon. Be quick and be alert; do exactly as the judge directs. Don't speak to him except to answer his questions. If he does something you don't like, don't say so. And don't irritate the judge (and everybody else) by constantly talking and fussing with your dog.

In moving about the ring, remember to keep clear of dogs beside you or in front of you. It is my advice to you *not* to show your Bichon in a regular point show until he is at least close to maturity and after both you and your dog have had time to perfect ring manners and poise in the match shows.

Conformation isn't the only type of competition in which Bichons participate and fare well. This Bichon clears a bar jump at an agility trial.

SUGGESTED READING

OTHER T.F.H. BOOKS ON THE BICHON FRISE

TS-245

The World of the Bichon Frise is the most current volume available on the breed. Written by longtime breed expert Anna Katherine Nicholas and illustrated by over 300 full-color photos, this book covers everything that Bichon owners and fanciers want to know about the breed. Breed history, famous champions, Bichons around the world, caring for a Bichon, and breeding are some of the topics included in this comprehensive volume. Miss Nicholas brings the breed to life with the knowledge and experience of many years as an author, judge, and Bichon authority.

TW-136

Written by respected Bichon breeder and judge Ann Hearn, *The Proper Care of Bichons Frises* is illustrated by over 200 full-color photos and covers all of the basics of Bichon ownership. Bringing a new puppy home, keeping an adult Bichon vibrant and healthy, and everything in between is discussed in this informative work. The added insight of the author's personal perspective makes this book a must-have for every Bichon owner.